Dear Selection Committee

Praise for Dear Selection Committee

"I buried // everything they told me to bury. Then, I dug it up again," Melissa Studdard writes in *Dear Selection Committee*, an apt description of the work these poems do to unearth the incorrigible self and bury conventionality and its offspring, shame. The speaker revels in her largesse, claiming, in one poem's title, she's "Huge Like King Kong, Like Godzilla, Like Gulliver," and that the "world is my diorama of a world," and in another, that her honeymoon pictures are "the cover / of the 1855 edition of Leaves of Grass." All of this immensity, this grand unburying, is squeezed into the prosaic corseting structure of a job application, intensifying the split between tame and wild. Even her own birth is enacted with kinetic magnificence: "I broke the kingdom inside her, broke the gala / of horses straining to get out. I broke the dancehall // mirrors and even the gilded faucet handles. / I was a river that strong. Made for flooding." Indeed, these poems are so desirous and animated that they spilled over the edges of the page and into my thirsty soul.

—Diane Seuss

The poems in *Dear Selection Committee* say what I've always wanted to say in a job application (and what I'm thinking as I perform the role of Normal Job Person) but never had the guts. Melissa Studdard's burn-it-down-radical honesty is elating af—exactly what I needed to read—but the poetic attentiveness, from the first page to the last, was the real thrill. At the heart of the cyclone, a dependable, deepening pulse of self-preservation.

—Jennifer L. Knox

In the universe of Melissa Studdard's poems, both the speaker and the audience will always have their cake and eat it too. After all, "Life's never dull when your name's Melissa," and oh my goddess, does *Dear Selection Committee* serve hard as a brilliant 21st century take and critique of the epistolary, filled with infinite heart and infinite humor and infinite neon signs that point towards the larger-than-life nature of poetry. This is excess. This is extravagance. This is the definition of sensuality. Studdard has the tremendous gift of finding the center of every poem, giving us the whole damn thing.

—Dorothy Chan

Books by Melissa Studdard

Poetry

I Ate the Cosmos for Breakfast
Like a Bird with a Thousand Wings

YA Fiction

Six Weeks to Yehidah

Interviews

The Tiferet Talk Interviews

For Joan – With gratitude for your powerful words and heart of clarity –

Dear Selection Committee

Melissa Studdard

JACKLEG PRESS

JackLeg Press
www.jacklegpress.org

www.melissastuddard.com

ISBN: 978-1-7375134-1-4

Library of Congress Control Number: 2022931592

Cover design by Richard Every.
Cover art, *It is Easy to Type*, by Karyna McGlynn.

Dear Selection Committee,

I would like to be considered for the position
of drinking a bottle of chardonnay every night
and then making love with the most beautiful
person I know until we both pass out. I would
like to also request as little talking as possible
between the hours of legs open and legs closed.
If hired, I will need some important but modest
accommodations, such as mornings free of any
obligations and afternoons scheduled to practice
my Kegel exercises and rehydrate. I would prefer
an office with a view overlooking the most intriguing
mysteries of the universe, but I will settle for a small
window into the mind of God, so long as I have
curtains to pull closed when it gets too awkward.
I have no previous experience, but I am a quick
learner and an expert self-starter. My recommenders
will tell you, I am certain, that I am the most adept
person they know when it comes to finding hidden
value in hungover calculations of hours remaining
until bedtime. Please do not hesitate to be in touch
if you would like a sample of my creative work,
which was produced in collaboration with the only
other person I know who might be qualified for this
job—which I mention just in case another position
opens up before your application window closes.
I am attaching my resume, which is pheromone
scented for your olfactory pleasure and which
surely, you will agree, merits a possibly premature,
but unanimous, and wholly sincere, victory toast.

For Saint MSCT

CONTENTS

Is There Anything Else You Would Like the Committee to Know?

PART I: APPLICATION

Personal Statement

My Kind

My life's burning.
That's what I mean when they ask how I am and I say
Fine. Rope-dangling, kicking-the-chair-out-from-under-me
fine; flirting-with-blades fine; looking-for-Pallas-Athena-
in-my-pancake fine (why would she visit that twerp Telemachus
and not me?) In my spare time, I'm building a death out of sad
songs and leftover, microwavable food. I'm building a life
out of sad songs, good friends, and leftover microwavable food.
It occurs to me that I may be my own soul mate. That's how I've
ended up in this body alone. But science says self is not
so simple. I'm a mosaic of viruses, bacteria, and, likely, other
people. All of us making decisions together. Group hug!
I am my own kind. I'll learn to play piano. Like Hélène Grimaud,
I'll see blue rising from the notes. I'll be an amateur bird watcher,
a volunteer firefighter, a gourmet chef, a great
humanitarian. I'll plant a prize-winning garden,
grow a pot farm. My hair is on fire. I'm running
out of time. Maybe I'll learn to paint. Get
a cat or dog. Something sweet
that likes to cuddle and poops outside the house. Something
feral and one step from wild. Something that,
when the moon jumps in the lake,
will jump in after, howling, in awe of the lake,
in awe of the moon, in awe of itself and every other
disappearing thing.
My kind.

Family Tree

My mother was a lake
        full of water lilies,

my father was a bridge
        between the bardo

and heaven. He tossed me
        to his shoulders

for the parade of grandparents
        at night: Orion

and Cassiopeia, Gemini and Auriga.
        Once we saw a cousin

shoot from the ground beside
        a circle of pines. *Geyser,*

Mother said, tossing a silver
        carp into the air. When

I was old enough, I asked them
        the story of my birth,

and they each handed me a singing
        sparrow the color of my hair.

What Sets Me Apart
from Other Applicants

Flamboyant

You don't believe me when I say I'm coming
      to meet you at the park with my huge

homosexual umbrella. But you'll see,
      when I open it and twirl between

the obelisk and bamboo, you'll see
      how it flirts with other rainbow-colored

umbrellas, how it speeds up the pacemakers
      of passersby. My umbrella is so fine

that the pigeons have learned to talk, just
      so they can tell each other not to crap on it.

So fine that when the clouds see it,
      they open up their mouths and spill out

diamonds. The clouds don't even remember
      what rain is, and they recalibrate their drift

to match the pace at which my umbrella
      moves its sexy body along the sidewalk.

People have tried to call it *fabulous,* but *fabulous,*
      after all, is just a word,

and there are no words flamboyant enough
      for my huge homosexual umbrella.

Not even the words in this poem. Not even
    the words *huge homosexual umbrella,*

which, like the umbrella itself, may bring some
    joy, but unlike the real thing, will never

call you *honey doll* and hug you against the sunset
    in their bodacious gay arms.

Fascinating, the Parts of Us

that attain immortality before we do,
as if we'd sculpted ourselves into skyline against the first

gasp of night. I want to steal the hair
of everyone I've ever kissed, shave it right onto the pillow

from their unsuspecting sleep,
then carry it to the top floor of my obsession. I have trouble

letting go, it's true. In an elevator,
I'm the last to push my floor, and I drink five bottles

of water at a time, scattered all over
the house, afraid that if I finish them, I'll die. Same with books.

Lately I've been reading
about President Antonio López de Santa Anna, who ordered

a full military burial for his
amputated leg. He dug it up to transport from one home

to another, paraded it in an ornate royal
coach. I dream of sparrows lifting the ten pounds I lost last spring

to the sun, pinking
the edges of the city with what I used to be. Body that I can barely

keep up with, you owe me
nothing, not even your parts. Yet, I'm so hungry for the vanishing

lamps of your intelligence, I could
eat my own tail, I could pull my own lightning from the sky.

Contact Information

Untitled

My address is nostalgia
for things that never happened. I wander in
and out of coincidence, dragging a wagonful
of unrequited lovers behind me. I visit
the infirmary for broken
planets and ill poets, where I bandage
metaphors and remove stitches from busted
couplets. All will be well again—poets
restored to their regular neurotic tendencies,
free to enter emotional and psychological
terrain that would make others
run panicked from the landslides
in their own minds. Oh—what we embrace
to avoid the life we've been given. Oh—
what we embrace to live the life we've been given.
Call everything you've ever done
Untitled. It's the only honest way to create. Generate
a disaster in your life to sidestep
the true catastrophe of your life. Oh—there's a universe
with a bell around its neck, purring outside
your bedroom door. Let
it in. Oh—I tried to make this about you,
but it's about me me me.
My awful claws. My electric arch. Bats and blue jays
hunted from trees. I thought
I was good, but I never was. I'm coming home
with a bleeding angel
between my teeth. Open the door to the heart's door.
Imperfection is the only
muse. And I am her handmaiden. Please
love me anyway.

Inside the Beige Brick House, the Beige Rooms

and beige-shirted people sit beautiful as unbuttered
biscuits, their awful loveliness upon me. They want me

drier than wheat and so still no marbles can roll

from my head. I want summer flashing the yard
red with begonias. I want Ladder-backed Woodpeckers

knocking at the gables, and Crepe Myrtle blossoms

blown down like hot pink cotton in a storm.
I'm embarrassing like that. A walking faux pas no one

wants to be seen with at the mall. I know compassion

like the arms of a cactus. I know the scent of earth
revealing her secrets after a much-needed rain. I buried

everything they told me to bury. Then, I dug it up again.

In the House, I Built Another House

and that was my body,
made of wine, pills, and regret.
Made of cigarettes and self-blame.
Smoke and baby cries
leaked from all the windows.
The baby's face was a red fist
punching nothing.
Then the doctor said *pregnant*,
and I said I'll never be good enough.
And the doctor said,
The baby is not yet a baby.
I said, *I am the baby.*
I went home and built another house,
one that my husband could not enter.
A fortress of withdrawal.
He drank for both of us.
I started making bones.

Why I Want the Job

The Heart is a Muscular Organ

Each morning when I wake I pray
to be a channel of divine blessings to all I encounter.
By noon I'm pissed off at someone,
and, like a chopper full of soldiers, I carry God inside me.
They're dressed in camo and boots, haven't
bathed in a week, can't quite remember
how they got there. By dusk
I've bathed them a hundred times in the hidden
glow of compassion, changed them
out of camo into cool pastels,
unlaced the fighter boots and re-strapped the sandals.
My heart then is like a little forest clearing with the one
patch of sun shining on the people who piss me off.
The truth is sometimes I get tired of being human,
and I walk through the darkest part of my aorta,
collecting tiny flowers that grow hidden
under rocks and leaves the size of giants' feet.
This is how I learn to pray.
O God, I say, *let me be devoured by a pride of lions.*
O Lord, *please let me be reborn as strength.*

Sometimes My Body Forgets It's Not a Peacock

and struts through narrow streets fanning its extravagant
plumage. When I remind it to be human,
it laughs and winks its hundred eyes.
My fortune cookie says to marry the next
person I kiss, but I want to have my fortune and eat it too,
so I kiss an entire shopping mall full of people.
The truth is I crave both winter and summer, fall
and the excess pinks of spring. I hoard
snow boots and squirt guns,
surf boards and the gardens that bloom inside my head.
All the trench coats I own, I've embezzled
from myself. When fog
steals the things I covet, I hunt down
its opaque ass, kiss it on the lips,
and make love to it
before taking my things back
inside a crushed velvet bag
that I am also infatuated with. When waves
lick up the sandals I adore, I dive in and swim until
I'm a tangle of seaweed and froth,
and then I let the tongue of sea devour me,
which doesn't ever feel like cheating
though I'm smitten with two men,
one woman, and a non-binary
acquaintance. And sadly,
that makes me less
queer than I thought,
but I'm happy to still be on the continuum.
There can never be too many falling stars,
too many starlings, or blueberries, or foxes.
You must agree. Everyone's wild about foxes!
Until it's spring and lambs romp through fields
eating clover and forbs. Oh, don't make me choose.

I want to take them all home. So, I'll just
move my furniture to the field instead, and meteorologists
will promise that it'll never rain again anywhere I stand.
I'll buy all the lambs little
hats for our housewarming party. I'll buy the foxes
diamond necklaces
and mirrors to distract them from the lambs. O,
my little rainbows! My little strange pets! If the fawn
comes leaping over the heartberry bush,
can the love song be far behind?

A Little Bit Rain

It seemed this bicycle was faster
when I first started. Now the afterlife
is gaining on me, and every billboard I pass

has the same five words. I know
you'd like to know what they say, but
if you're ever going to build up those quads,

you'll to need to enter this race yourself.
I even hired the Rockettes to adorn the finish line
with their legs. All for you. That's how much

I love you. The moon used to be yellow,
but I painted it green for your green-loving eyes,
then left a pack of cigarettes and two aspirin

on the nightstand. Maybe don't get so drunk
next time, okay? I like it when you do that thing
with your tongue. It makes me want to get

matching tattoos. We could translate our bodies
into a new language. Your mouth a little
bit summer. My mouth a little bit rain.

Relevant Experience

Did I Do, O God, Did I As I Said I'd Do? Good! I Did.

between my thighs
    where my love is always requited
        where the dark bell forgot how to sleep
            where the hundred-year flower blooms
                too close to the cliff
                    I found lost worlds
                      and their sweet ruinations
                            slick and tender as half-eaten plums
                                  I found small cities covered in ash
                        the diverging and converging of
                tectonic plates
                  beneath a forgotten sea
                and the island where I'd exiled all my fears
              reaching slantwise for light

    from my center

        reaching slantwise for light
            and the island where I'd exiled all my fears
              beneath a forgotten sea
                  the diverging and converging of
                    tectonic plates
                    I found small cities covered in ash
                slick and tender as half-eaten plums
            and their sweet ruinations
            I found lost worlds
        too close to the cliff
      where the hundred-year flower blooms
    where the dark bell forgot how to sleep
  where my love is always requited
between my thighs

Planted My Shame in the Backyard

Planted its bones beneath a blooming magnolia. Carried its head
past a split of fence. Did not ask why
the shine of remaining alive. Instead walked filthy
with my hands full of prayers. Delivered their blood
to the flask of shadow. Planted knuckles
and shinbones. Shoveled soil over
shards of the coffee cup
hurled at my face. Buried spatulas and gin bottles
and broken lamps. Used the flat
side of the shovel to pound it all down
into the loamy gash
holy dark as my woman gash
that has swallowed
and swallowed
to no avail
the fevers of this world.

Recommenders

The Angel

It was this beautiful little sorrow-soft
duck with 1950's-aqua-appliance-colored
feet, and it quacked like a firecracker going off

and pulled my mind from worry out to
wobble and wade. The sun hung like
a disco ball over the lake, so the duck made

merry and took me with her. I was competing
about something financial, but the duck's
extraordinary luck made me say *No man,*

this shit won't fly and I figured out a way to create
a lucrative passive income flow so instead of
defeating the people, I could tell everyone

how to do it, how to get rich and spend their time
at the pond looking at ducks instead of working,
working, working, and we compared notes

on the iridescence of feather, and because oats
are way better for ducks than bread, we invested
in organic oatmeal, and somewhere along the way

someone gave me a necklace made out of real
stars because when you're rich and have a direct line
to aqua-footed duck angels, you can do that. Let me

tell you I've been having the same dream for fifteen
years. A think tank of 72 people asking whether
language is an instrument of thought or a mold for it.

We call ourselves *The Poets* and we're allergic
to reason, which never brought anyone
anything good, with the exception of Foucault,

who rejected labels but was infected by a predilection
for thinking about finitude instead of ducks. And, who
is this *man* Foucault refers to anyway? What part of him

is woman? And, what are we standing on when we say
Earth? Whose back? Who has to work when we
don't work? I'm grabbing my shovel. I love you.

When the Drunk Guy Sent an Injured Baby Goldfinch to the Wildlife Rehab by Uber

My kid DM'd me two smileys laughing tears
and the note: *This is something you would do,*

and I don't know if that meant the drunk part

or the goldfinch alone in the backseat part
but I think it's possible life may just be

God telling a series of knock knock jokes

so I run to answer the door
and a golden flower blooms in my chest

and I call it *laughter*

and I delight in how my kid takes time to message me
and a bouquet of silver flowers blooms in my chest

and I call it *having a kid who DM's me*

and another bouquet of flowers blooms in my chest
and I pluck them and hand them to a homeless man

and they regrow

and I pluck them and hand them to a robin's nest
and they flutter down into the air around me

and I am a flutter among them

dancing on a picnic table at the park
and I send a video of it to everyone I know

and my kid is the first to respond

and I am a thousand barrels of wine
pouring myself into the world

Education & Formal Training

My Boyfriend's Body's Covered in Newspaper

And the headline says,
Penis-Shaped Subtropical Storm Melissa

Arouses Commentary On Twitter.
And I'm like, *I told you.*

And he's like, *Will you still love me*
when my shoreline starts eroding?

Life's never dull when your name's
Melissa and your mascot

is a huge, erect, disembodied penis
hovering over the Atlantic.

Which is to say, *absofuckinglutely*—
I'll still love you. What surprises me

about the body is resilience. Mine
has been a shot glass, a punching

bag, a cigarette filter, a lie
detector, a crash test dummy.

Oh, how it opens and opens anyway
when passion comes near. So I rain

seven days and seven nights
inside the penis outline.

I whisper the safe word
to the ocean, in case it's had enough.

And when my beloved asks
what time I'll be over,

I say, *I'd travel a thousand years
for one night of this wonder.*

Wrap It in Silk

And give it to the dead—the wound
the doctors can't repair. Because the ribs

are a curve in promise

to the lungs, and the lungs are blessings
that fill you with sky.

Breathe into the machine as if you're

not broken. Breathe as if freeway
and headlights aren't lodged

beneath your skin. Breathe

as if your radio hasn't given up song
to siren. Ask about your kids

in the room across the hall. Try to stay

awake to hear the doctor's response.
Google *ribs and broken,* but don't

read the warnings spread out

before you or the articles about Vikings
and Blood Eagle torture. Don't imagine

how, with wings like that, you could fly. Drive

on the frontage road for an entire
year. Drive home and home and home

until you remember who holds you.

The Pain Is So Resplendent It Has Babies

and its babies are so resplendent
they have babies. Underage unwed
babies having babies. Someone has
built their delivery room in my ribs,
and without restraint, they come and go
carrying babies that will birth more
babies in the parking lot before realizing
they are babies. Flamboyant babies,
refusing the swaddle of pink and blue.
They leave the hospital in sequined
evening gowns to perform the burlesque
of pain, and everyone in the audience
has their shirts unbuttoned to nurse
the babies they carry everywhere.
And the speakers, instead of making
sound, make babies, and the curtains
open and close on a pulley of pain
operated by the babies, and when
the magician comes onstage she saws the pain
in half and there are two more pains that
saw themselves in half and now the pain
knows how to saw itself to make more
pain and there are pain babies everywhere
and there are no rabbits or doves in the hat,
just more babies, and when the cocktail
waitress comes around, she serves
little cups of pain, shots of pain with pain
backs on the rocks, and pain crudités
on leafy green beds of pain, and when
I try to leave the show to go home
the emcee announces my next set,
and I realize it was just me onstage
all along, having babies and babies
and more babies with no epidurals.
I realize it is me who has conceived, and
mothered, and nurtured, my pain all along.

Honors & Awards

Huge Like King Kong, Like Godzilla, Like Gulliver in the Land of Lilliput,

Like Zsa Zsa Gabor's fingernails, like Julia Roberts' smile—so huge
I don't have to waste any more energy growing and can spend all
my time admiring myself in internet searches and Chateau-sur-Mer
mirrors. When I walk through town, no one can believe how big
I am. My feet would crush them if they didn't get out of the way.
And my hands, they're so big you would think they were tree branches,
except my fingers don't sway in the wind. When I go into a restaurant,
the manager has to saw off the roof just so I can fit inside. I wear
a convertible Mercedes for a hat. I wear chandeliers as bangles.
When I wash my face, I use an entire lake. My house has its own
zip code, school district, and homeowner's association. My cats
manage their own salmon-canning factory. The world is their
litter box. The world is my diorama of a world. If you wonder
why I'm writing, it's just to say a big THANK YOU
to everyone who nominated me for the award and to show
you how deserving I am. If selected, I will make you
proud. I will pull down the sky and give it to you as a scarf.
I will give you an entire meadow for your yoga mat and morning
stretches. I will turn your debt into diamonds, your pet's dung
into dungarees. So, remember, my darling, my infinitely sensible,
my deliciously judicious friends, when you've got that ballot in your
tiny little hand, do yourself a favor, make yourself bigger, vote for ME.

At Fifty, I Became a Three-Time Finalist for the Darwin Awards

Crashed my car into myself and climbed out of both
into my other flame, to burn, a genius of not leaving.
The freeway said *there's a hole in time's pocket, a weather
system, drunk gamblers who won't stay put at the casino,*

and I said *take me to the glass hour, the sliver and sleet.
Take me.* My wings were born in a miniature coffin.
They found their song in my broken throat,
at the bottom of an empty smile. I chased them

across a continent and slipped on the concrete,
cracked my head on mortality's countertop, ended
up with a concussion full of mismatched words
and poor judgements. Just a few weeks after, I dived

into a bacteria-laden no swim advisory. There were no
buoys, but I kept my death in a small gift basket,
covered, and saved for later, the way we save what is
most precious to us, the things we're most likely to forget.

Job Objectives

To Be with Trees

I dreamed of trees with blue veins in a forest full of wilting.
And there, all my southern girl self, full of *No thank yous,*

full of *You first* and *Go ahead and have the last piece of cake.*

I *want* that last piece of cake. Dreamed the trees
made me my own torte, and I could have the whole thing.

My sisters, the trees, they said *Come now, sit, eat.*

They had blue veins in the forest full of wilting, and I cried.
There were no forks. They said my hands were fork enough.

And when I tried to say *please,* the trees said my eyes

were *please,* and they said my mouth was *thank you,*
and the trees cried too. They had beautiful eyes

for crying. A color I had never seen. So I named it

Godlovesyoureyesbecausetheymadethemthisbeautifulcolor.
Now anyone who ever saw the color would think of the trees

and the meaning of the trees, which was to be.

Migration Patterns

In the dream I tell customs my llama is a goat.
Because sometimes the heart is not large

enough to hold what is beautiful
if the mind finds it exotic. Sometimes the mind

mistakes itself for a hoarded piece of land
and little campfires spring up everywhere. Smoke

slinks through chain link. Small hands and shoulders
capsize beneath a dehydrated, salt-sick

sun. In the dream I carry mountains through
international waters. I carry the hills, their babies,

to safety. Sometimes I wave away a predator
and there is fire in my hand and my hand

does not want to be part of a human body.
It wants to belong to the llama, the goat, the hills,

the mountain. In the dream I've got the North Star
in my trunk. I'm driving it across a border.

I'm taking it to a different part of the sky. It can't
stand what it has seen. What we need

is not a fixed point. What we need is a world
anthem that everyone knows the words to, one

that says, *Come in, come on, come over. I've got you.*
In the dream light leaks from thin cracks

where the trunk door meets the body of the car.
The star says, *Put me on the dashboard, and I will guide*

you. The officer says, *Illegal. You can't take a star*
to another part of the sky. And I say, *Watch me.*

I say, *I've got enough light to do anything.*

PART II: INTERVIEW

List Obstacles and Challenges You've Faced, and if Applicable, How You Overcame Them

Hurricane, 3rd Day

We hid in the belly of porcelain. The world
sang sirens overlapping, the sound of wind

taking gates from the hinge. That whistling, yes.
Whistling and whipping, the world the cry

of a cow caught in the spin of a twister and lifted.
Water creeping to the back door like a thief.

It wanted the jewels of our eyes.

In the house next door, a woman breastfed
another woman's baby, the thin-sweet milk.

Across the street, a man wrote social security numbers
On his kids' arms with a Sharpie—*a game,* he said.

And in our tub, we held the news in our palms:

forty dogs from a kennel rescued by boat, a guy
on paddleboard heaving toddlers from a window, one

by one. And trapped across town, a shop full
of bakers sleeping on flour sacks, baking all day—

they slept and baked, slept and sprinkled.
For whoever might need. Not even sampling

or licking a finger. Once, I thought humankind
brutal and nature benign—foolish child

with my frog in a box, my holey lid.
Once, before, I asked to be delivered.

O sugar-hungry God, the world
has been dredged and is waiting.

Life Is the Saddest Thing That Ever Happened to Me

As it turns out, I was the party
waiting to happen, and my mother,

she was the corridor to the clubhouse,
narrow and occult, filled with the scent of light.

I broke the kingdom inside her, broke the gala
of horses straining to get out. I broke the dancehall

mirrors and even the gilded faucet handles.
I was a river that strong. Made for flooding.

On the other side, the game had already started:
The family-in-waiting hot in a match of Scrabble.

I broke the letters, broke the game
board, broke, with my cry, the need

for speech. Only the nurse knew what to say: *Here,*
Sweetie, placing me at my mother's

breast. In *The Book of Letters*, Rabbi Kushner says
the OTIYOT exist independent of ink or paper

or words, says when Moses shattered the first
set of tablets, the letters ascended

to *The One Who Gave Them.* So, this is how
we arrive in this life: already letting go, mystical

as the ALEF-BEIT, independent of mothers, fathers
and bodies, casting our own incomprehensible,

immortal spells—flying back, already flying back,
into the feathery, hollow-boned throat of God.

Everyone in Me Is a Bird

Mind was a prison, ruby lined
in its lipstick noir—everything woman
I was expected to be, trapped between
papered walls. What they said to do, I did not

but only levitated at the burning, the body

a water in which I drowned, the life
a windshield dirty with love. What they
said to think, I thought not but instead made
my mind into a birdcage with wings.

What Are Some Errors You Made in Previous Jobs That You'd Like to Avoid Repeating?

Tour of Grief

All seventeen days the orca wore
her dead like a crown,

sorrow riling to a bob and weave,
knocking her hollow.

What water and womb
could no longer carry, she had to carry.

We watched through binoculars
as if distance

were real. As if
we were not also tottering

on the head of an exhausted,
grieving mother. As if we were not also

becoming too cumbersome,
too heavy to bear.

Group Portrait with Trophy Kill

As if cupping a palm leaf, we drank from it,
drank the stars from its belly, slurped the spongy
marrow from its bones. We drank and ate lava
from the curves of its shoulders, holding firm so
we could snap back its head and lick the sweat
from its neck. We cracked the coconuts
of its eyes and cut rivers of sandy milk from them,
rivers which we drank and drank, chewing
on the milk-fattened fish and nipples. It grew
thorns and we ate them with butter. It crouched
like a skunk, and we ate its stink, ate the fear
it secreted. We boiled its blood for the marinade
that we brushed back onto the skewered bits
of its body. We ate it all and ate it all, and when
it said it had no more we made it breed and ate
its offspring and drank the love it lactated
for them. Finally, it released a poison, and we
ate its poison on everything, lapping up the fat the way
you do a golden yolk—on bread, on ham, on pancakes—
on your own finger, when nothing else is left.

How Would Past Colleagues Describe What It's Like to Work with You?

We Made a Gala

I've lived 7,000 years already.
5,000 of them in countries I've never visited.
This century is the conversation that disrupts
my heart. We've eaten a plate of fiasco,
a paint-by-numbers pandemic
of pandemonium proportions, 1,000 pans of egg rice.
I'd show you the world as I see it, but that might
shatter your preconceived notions
and how would we repair that? The truth is, God's sweet on
the magpies and the miniscule, and Eve
never bit any apple. She wore a hat made of honey
and danced like a wood nymph
through the orchard of history, so the orchard
wilted beneath her beauty. When fear
becomes irrational we nickname it *woman, apple,*
snake, breasts. I can't answer your questions, but I can
bless your dirty laundry and tell you
sin's secrets. And, yes, safety is a luxury, but maybe
we humans deserve it—so I mix memory with vodka
and call it a highball.
I walk through the meadows of suffering,
the parking lots of wonder. When the funeral comes, it will
not be for the living,
it will be for us. I am singing a song for you,
reading the century's eulogy. Weren't we terrific?
We made a gala in our suits made of skin.

The Continent Expanding in You

It's easy to love a lot of people at once.

Because.

The glass breaking could reveal
wound or it could reveal brilliance.

Sadness, lust, and awe
walk into a bar. One
reaches for the ashtray. One orders a gin.
One falls in love with the streetlamp's
reflection in the window.

The underworld is the overworld,
and the overworld is the inbetweenworld,
and the inbetweenworld
is also the alsoworld.

It's all so much.

You should be careful
when you pray for abundance.

Do you know
how to properly fold it?

Do you know
that the eye of a needle
is a planet made of light?

You Say Cognitive Dissonance, I Say I Lost My Basket Full of Light

We eat sweetness, and that's it. We don't just
make lemons
into lemonade. We make them into
adult beverages featuring
lemonade,
or popsicles, or lemon meringue pie.
We worship in line
at Costco, where we find 7,000 boxes
of enlightenment, nutrition labeled.
We worship in an empty lot
where lime green frogs call to lime
green birds across a dry cleaner's
parking spot. When we cross
and uncross our legs,
we unleash our melodies
the way a sigh out of rhythm
with the rest of the breath
becomes a bluebird
flying into another color. The truth is
we are really just here to revive
each other's dreams, to tap
the anthem of survival
on our pots and pans,
in sync, from our balconies.
I dream of boxes that don't need
to be sprayed with Lysol
before the music stops playing.
I dream of workers who return

and return to redo the same job
the way I train my mind
repeatedly to a peace
I am making up as I go along.
Once, it seemed life was for
touching others. Now we know
just how far apart we can stand
and still be in love.

How Do You Take Responsibility for Your Role in Mistakes and Conflicts?

When We Fuck Up, Which Is Often

We pretend life's a sitcom, and then it's funny that I spent
the evening buzzed on Facebook and now have 3 new
contests to judge and 2 new boyfriends, funny that you hit
reply all in your message meant for me—saying you would
screw 12 of the 20 class moms but only 7 of the dads,
funny—YES—that you listed them by name, categorized
them by asset. You like your tragedies like you like your
gadgets—grotesquely lavish, rhinestone-studded and endlessly
refracting. It's true we never auditioned for this show, but
here we are, anyway, killing it with lines that slide open
like the bellies of drones just as the pilot realizes she has
the wrong coordinates. We like to imagine we have settings
like blow driers: cool, medium, and hot—and we can
adjust at will, but the next thing we know one of us has spilled
a bag of potato chips, a Grande Iced Cinnamon Dolce Latte,
and a smoked mozzarella sandwich, pesto side down,
on the entryway floor of the producer's apartment. Or thrown
up pizza on the director's shoes. Door #3 makes us feel better,
so we take it, but the prize is behind Door #2. That's funny!
Right? Hello, signal laugh track. The runs in our pantyhose
are cute. The bad highlights? Hilarious. We wear our clumsiness
like badges. We're relatable that way, adored by audiences.
When it's time to renew our contracts, they'll add extra
seasons, knowing, as everyone who watches our show
knows, we can sustain our mistake-making for so long,
with such extravagance, we can entertain you forever.

I Have an Apology, 6 Requests, and 4 Offers (But Not in That Order)

Dear people, sorry I didn't make it
                              to my reading tonight
but I finally tried
                    the medical marijuana I

        bought in Aspen this summer

and accidentally spent the evening dancing flamenco

        with my cats

who by the way

                think I am quite good

and by the way I am a tulip now and if you want to come to my

                                next event

        I will try to make sure someone moves the pot

                that holds me

into the sunlight because the event is
                                watching me grow

        please bring your watering cans and fertilizer

plants adore being tended and spoken to

                I run back and forth inside the soil

looking for a sign that I exist

               so if you could take pictures of me

and post them on the internet I would

                       appreciate it

        and please clap when I unfurl

     it may be slow and difficult to discern with the naked eye

but unfurling is hard work, and if it's too much trouble

          for you to watch with just your eyes

I can provide

telescopes or microscopes or whatever will help you see me

                better

        because I am super

                       hot for a tulip

and I'm sure you will want to see

               I can

as well

     provide pamphlets that diagram this

revolution which

           if no one has informed you

costs 2 bottles of wine per participant

please pour them directly onto my foliage

I prefer white but I will drink

whatever

and if you are also a tulip and have no hands to pour with

I can offer you

a sexy little mitten

that thinks it is a hand and will pour for you

I realize this is all somewhat

unexpected

but I also know that life is a bioluminescent fantasy

and it is so goddamn beautiful and if you

put your ear close to it

it sounds like Spanish guitar emanating

from a seashell

at least that's how it seems when you are a tulip

but please don't take my word for it

please go to the souvenir shop yourself and buy

a memento from earth

to remember all this sublime clicking after you die

                            I am willing to purchase at least two of

the postcards

            and one of the Mickey Mouse shot glasses

                                    myself

if only to ensure we can learn the art of screaming

            while stomping along the beach on top of seashells

some people say we are destructive

                            but I say

        we are making sand

What Are Some Important Lessons You Have Learned from Previous Jobs?

Revolution in C Minor

While democracy is a pigeon
    looking for a landing,
        consumerism is an accident

from when God fell asleep.
    Now the skyline is inside me
        like a door leading to someone

else's bedroom. Nothing on the dresser
    is mine. The ornate gold frames
        hold other people's children,

the jewelry box—someone else's jade.
    I move across the carpet
        in my slippers and mist, a myth

not yet written. What it is I want
    to become, no man can answer
        or buy. It's possible

I'm the mother of vast, dark silences.
    It's possible I will grandparent
        a litter of storms.

Deathbolts Illuminate the Wonderstorm

Cruel, the highway that
took the dogs.

I've seen its shoulders
convulse gently in the crying of nightfall

the way a teenaged girl can be
both vicious and vulnerable.

It doesn't like what it has done,
and I don't like to say it.

Sometimes I hold a kaleidoscope
to my beloved's eye
and ask him
to never look at anything again
but me.

How can I trust a world
that hasn't yet
honored the softness in his pupil?

Is it possible to protect those we care for?
To protect anyone?

I plant plum trees in his heart.
I devour his fruits to the pit.

Love is sometimes a stay
against insanity.

The dogs, it was my fault.
Trying to help, I scared them
into the rush.

I live it over and over.
The way a body can spill
like sunlight
from its skin.

If Falling Is a Leaf

urging the earth
into autumn
the branch is a lover who remembers
orange unlocked at the gates of fire

orange so bold it seduces green

orange unbuttoning the sun
and wearing it to summer's funeral

because in loss
we are most vibrant

because urgent regions
of the leaf's mind
ignite only when it opens
to its own demise

all foliage
is reincarnated into desire

and we're slayed
by light coming in
through a kitchen window

as though we hadn't already seen it
for decades through the same pane

so we sneak to the coatroom
of our own party to make love
in everyone else's fur

feral but divine

our behavior is not wholly holy
but the trees

oh my God

they wear their hearts on their leaves

Will You Need Any Special
Accommodations or Supplies?

When I Say What for the Tenth Time in an Hour, You Ask if I Know What Happened to Beethoven's Hearing

and I say maybe it was a little Violet-backed Starling
flew into his ear and got trapped and all he could hear
after that was birdsong

and you're like nope, and I'm like but wouldn't that be
unbearably beautiful like the little stars you see

when you get whacked upside the head,
and you're like guess again,

so I wonder
if his nose just got tired
and wanted to quit smelling
and his ears
joined in solidarity

now you find an excuse to leave

the room and when you come back you're wearing
only a purple tie and I have the desire suddenly to chew
the legs off something like when Beethoven sawed

his piano to the floor to sound the boards

and pressed his ear to the mahogany plank
to make it an instrument
for measuring what drives a foot to dance

but you say keep going, guess again
and I'm like what do I get
what's the prize
so you lift your plum-colored tie as if
I didn't already know the notes rising from your chest
are a perfect steam

and I'm like okay I'll keep playing

and I wonder if the sun inside Beethoven's ears
set too early

and you say now that's just silly

and I say *olé* and make clapping in my head

now your hum is multiplying by autogamy
because I swear I did not pollinate
anything but there it is, the hum making
a kite of itself
and sailing across our ears

so I say maybe his hearing got lost
in the labyrinth of his ear

and you say getting warmer

and I say

lobe shot off in a duel

bad pierce job

wax job gone awry

someone mistook his ear
for a crystal dish and poured in a fondue

no?
okay

too many years of weighty eyeglasses
broke his listen

his hearing went to heaven before him to

turn back his bedsheets and fluff
his pillow

and you say how have we even had this
conversation considering you quit talking

a week ago,

and I say sometimes
it's exactly what we lost
that makes us amazing

so you tell me Beethoven
poured ice water over his head
just enough years in a row
to freeze out his hearing

and I say I don't ever want
to get over this laryngitis

and you say *duende*

and I say carry me
to the bedroom
carry me to the bedroom
and don't ever leave my bed

Supplies I Will Require Before Seriously Considering the Job

1	horse that says it's a unicorn
3	guitars tuned to the melancholy of my childhood
6	ceremonial washing jugs whose bellies have held water turned into wine
2	rocks that were made into pets and given names
1	treatise over the impact of human behavior on the mental health of angels
7	dandelion puffs that were chased by leopard cubs
9	exegeses interpreting the lamplight scrawled across my boyfriend's body
12	polka dots exiled for being too exciting for their fabric
4	Bohemian waxwings willing to serve as proxies for all meetings before 11 a.m.
7	imaginary tea sets used in underwater tea parties
1	email filter that bounces back any message trying to assign a task
2	compasses set to the longing of Odysseus' nostalgia
1	saint reincarnated into a valentine and slipped beneath my bedroom door
2	sleepwalking tambourines bound with lust-colored ribbons
3	strands of hair from a woman who believes the horse

How Will You Demonstrate Your Commitment to the Company?

Incantation

—*for Paige and Kaveh*

Speaking of vows, someone mailed the bride
an envelope filled with finch's wings. As if marriage
could ever be so simple. The groom said, *Bring me
this new dialect. I want to fill it with couplets.* The bride said,
First, show me the ladder in your throat. When they handed
each other the promise, it looked like hoops of gold.
But really it was a sunrise that will go on and on. After all,
every poem is widest where it's been stretched by lovers
walking in twos. But this must be how all marriages begin:
someone carrying an envelope filled with enchantment,
someone opening it without breaking the wings.

When My Lover Says
Hippopotomonstrosesquippedaliophobia

I say, *it's not fear that matters, but where*
you bury it. So he buries his
tongue inside me, and I tell him that sometimes I'm more afraid
of hearing what I know
than knowing it. I want to lick the vowels out of all words
longer than three syllables. I want to find every horse
led against its will into battle and tie it to a cloud.
What sky said to the wind to make it bend the daffodils,
it also said to my lover's lips. So I turn
over and over
inside the field of myself. I offer
my flowers to his centerpiece,
my sunset to his lake. Tell me, who
never wakes up afraid?
The night before the crucifixion,
when Jesus asked if he really had to,
death showed up dressed in yellow petals
and handed him a crown of thorns. Don't make me
say what I'm willing to do for love.
I'm already lugging my cross up the hill.

Describe Your Management Style & How You Assign Tasks

Sensualists' Guide to the Apocalypse

Let's smoke pot and give each other
massages. Let's read *The Lover's Manual*
for Helping Goldfish Find Their Bowlmates
aloud to a restaurant full of waitresses and waiters. Let's
open our own café and serve only whipped cream
on the tips of penises. My plum, when I make
a statement about Cupid's body,
run behind me shouting to the press
that I'm a liar. Tell them
we've flown to France just to eat crème brûlée
out of little white ramekins. Let's rename
all the colors to confuse the painters and interior
decorators. No one will know what's
going to squeeze out of their master tubes,
and it will take them eternity
to sort it out. If I asked you
to make love with me
hanging from inversion bars in gravity boots,
would you? Let's climb Mount Vesuvius
while it's spewing
wearing nothing
but our immortality. If I
hand you a goldfish,
coo to it like a baby, and bathe it
in the Renaissance-gold light
of Leonardo da Vinci's mind.
O my sweet! Can the end ever really come
when it takes us four hours to eat a sandwich
because we have to stop seven times
to make love?

Modus Operandi

I put ranch dressing on the Greek salad. I stand
in my front yard in the rain and yell *I'm the biggest
waterfall in this desert.* When people invite me
to parties, I say *No* then show up anyway. I bring
my cat dressed in a graphic t-shirt with an image
of another, more attractive, cat. I tell everyone
I've just returned from my honeymoon, and when
they ask to see pictures, I show them the cover
of the 1855 edition of *Leaves of Grass.* I like kissing
people I don't know, sending flowers to random
addresses and signing the card *Eternally Yours, God.* I'm
a window cracked in the rain. My name is
Sitting Down and Standing Back Up for No Reason.
My motto is wings flapping. You should come back
into my room if you miss me. I'll be there soon.
I'm 1,000 miles away on a different bed.

Is There Anything Else You Would Like the Committee to Know?

Everyone Around Here Is Doing Their Best

The cat pooping on the floor, with every
part of his body but his butt in the litter box,
is doing his best.

The kids, who hate bathing
and smell like play-doh and earthworms,
are doing their best.

The purple-eyed fly crashing
over and over into the window
is doing its best.

The houseplants leaning in an unsightly
lack of symmetry towards the light
are doing their best.

The rug, about which lies were told,
and which is not, after all, stain proof,
is doing its best.

And even I,
though you may not believe it,
am doing my best.

We Either Will or Will Not

die in this moment
will or will not throw plastic into the ocean
will or will not tango
to the rumbling
hood of the car and call it leaning
will not or will throw
ourselves off the narrow edge of the universe
will or will not write the great American novel
will smoke pot or not or not or not
or will wreck the car will not will
leave all our belongings to a river we drank
and peed back into itself we will we will
staple ourselves back into the marrow
will dive deep into the hummingbird heart
learn to go faster we will or will not
we will will we
enter the anthropocene, half-opened,
catch space junk falling from
each other's mouths,
stomp stomp it out stomp the laugh
from the warbler,
write letters to the presidents of distant galaxies,
stay awake in the wind
that messed up the dandelion's hair
we will we will stomp morning
into the sun stomp the sun's face
into the basket we carry to gather
eggs will paint the eggs will or will not
take them to the church down the street
for kids who would otherwise have nothing
we will or will not remember the kids

will or will not take the eggs
the eggs that are fertilized
with the chickens'
sorrow and what
will happen to the kids
when they eat the chickens'
sorrow we either will or will not
notice will or will not make change,
we will will we not or will we
remark on what it all meant

All That's Left

Listen, the afternoon will soon fade into affliction
and we'll have no choice but to challenge gravity.
I've been corralling wind just for this. I wear it like
a lapel and when someone pays me a compliment
I play it back to them. Listen, the earth is burning
and all we have left is a plastic Jesus that lived up
to its promise to stay intact at any temperature,
through any catastrophe. If only I could get
a message to the owner of this apocalypse, I'd say
Go easier on the advertising. No one likes to see
zombies in Louboutin before breakfast. Listen,
it's just us here now. Give me your hand.

About the Author

Melissa Studdard is the author of five books, including the poetry collection *I Ate the Cosmos for Breakfast.* Her work has been published or featured by places such as NPR, PBS, *The New York Times, The Guardian,* POETRY, *Kenyon Review, Psychology Today,* and *New England Review.* Her awards include The Poetry Society of America's Lucille Medwick Memorial Award, *The Penn Review* Poetry Prize, the REEL Poetry Festival Audience Choice Award, the Tom Howard Prize, and more.

Notes

1. The title "My Kind" alludes to the title of the poem "Her Kind," by Anne Sexton.

2. On July 9th, 2019, while out drinking with friends, a man in Northern Utah discovered a struggling baby goldfinch, and too intoxicated to drive, saved it by sending it to the Wildlife Rehabilitation Center, alone, via Uber.

3. "Penis-Shaped Subtropical Storm Melissa Arouses Commentary On Twitter" was the title of many news headlines on October 11, 2019.

4. When the orca Tahlequah carried her dead calf for 17 days and 1, 000 miles, scientists referred to the journey as a "Tour of Grief," and the phrase was frequently referenced in news sources.

5. In the poem, "When My Lover Says *Hippopotomonstrosesquippedaliophobia,*" the lines "What sky said to the wind to make it bend the daffodils, / they also said to my lover's lips" are inspired by and structurally echo the Rumi poem "What was said to the Rose."

6. The title "Everyone in Me Is a Bird" comes from a line in an Anne Sexton poem.

Acknowledgments

With grateful acknowledgement to the directors, editors, publishers, judges, and staff of the organizations that featured the poems listed below, sometimes in different versions:

100 Poems to Save the Earth Anthology: "To Be with Trees"

Academy of American Poets, Poem-a Day: "Everyone in Me Is a Bird"

Aesthetica Creative Writing Anthology (Poetry Award Shortlist): "Fascinating, the Parts of Us"

Allentown Symphony (Performance): "If Falling Is a Leaf"

Conduit: "A Little Bit Rain"

Crosswinds Poetry Journal: "We Either Will or Will Not"

Cutthroat: "Inside the Beige Brick House, the Beige Rooms" and "Incantation"

The Dhaka Review: "My Kind," "We Either Will or Will Not," "The Heart Is a Muscular Organ," "Inside the Beige Brick House, the Beige Rooms" and "Incantation"

Hoxie Gorge Review: "Planted My Shame in the Backyard" and "We Made a Gala"

The Journal: "Revolution in C Minor"

Juxtaprose: "You Say Cognitive Dissonance, I Say I Lost My Basket Full of Light"

The Kenyon Review: "Tour of Grief"

Life and Legends: "Supplies I Will Require Before Seriously Considering the Job"

Missouri Review (Runner-up, Jeffrey E. Smith Editor's Prize): "Deathbolts Illuminate the Wonderstorm, " "I Have an Apology, 6 Requests, and 4 Offers (But Not in That Order)," "Dear Selection Committee," "Modus Operandi," and "All That's Left"

The Los Angeles Review: "Wrap It in Silk"

Moon City Review: "Then, Sometimes, My Body Forgets It's Not a Peacock" and "At Fifty, I Became a Three-Time Finalist for the Darwin Awards"

New Ohio Review: "Hurricane, 3rd Day" (special thanks to David Wanczyk for editorial insights)

The New Republic: "Group Portrait with Trophy Kill"

The New York Times: "Everyone in Me Is a Bird"

The Normal School: "My Kind"

Paws Healing the Earth Anthology: "Tour of Grief" and "Deathbolts Illuminate the Wonderstorm"

The Penn Review (The Penn Review Poetry Prize): "The Pain Is So Resplendent It Has Babies"

Poetry Daily: "Fascinating, the Parts of Us"

Poetry Society of America (Lucille Medwick Memorial Award for Poem on a Humanitarian Theme): "Migration Patterns"

Quiet Rooms Anthology: "Hurricane, 3rd Day"

Sequoyah Cherokee River Journal: "To Be With Trees," "Family Tree," "If Falling Is a Leaf" (special thanks to Mysti S. Milwee for translations into Cherokee Syllabary)

Skin Deep Anthology: "Family Tree"

Southword Journal (Gregory O'Donoghue Poetry Competition Finalist): "In the House, I Built Another House," and "When My Lover Says Hippopotomonstrosesquippedaliophobia"

SWIMM Miami (and Dolly's Florist and O'Miami Poetry Fest): "When the Drunk Guy Sent an Injured Baby Goldfinch to the Wildlife Rehab by Uber" in *SWWIM* daily, as a broadside, and delivered in bouquets as an origami flower

The Talking Gourds (Broadside for Telluride Arts): "All That's Left"

TAST: "Everyone in Me Is a Bird"

Telluride Institute (Fischer Prize Finalist): "Migration Patterns"

Tiferet Journal: "The Heart Is a Muscular Organ"

Tinderbox: "To Be with Trees" and "Life Is the Saddest Thing That Ever Happened to Me"

Verse Daily: "A Little Bit Rain"

Visible Poetry Project (short film by Pat van Boeckel): "To Be with Trees"

Waxwing: "Fascinating, the Parts of Us"

Winning Writer's Tom Howard Award: "Migration Patterns"

Witness Magazine: "When I Say What for the Tenth Time in an Hour, You Ask if I Know What Happened to Beethoven's Hearing"

I am grateful, as well, to the wonderful people of the Hermitage Artist Retreat (and Josip Novakovich), Centrum Residency, The Grind, and SWWIM Residency at The Betsy Hotel for the gifts of inspiration, time, and encouragement.

Huge thanks to the amazing people at JackLeg Press, especially Simone Muench, Jennifer Harris, Juan Felipe Herrera, and Ruben Quesada for early and enthusiastic support.

Endless gratitude to superstar friends Kelli Russell Agodon, Jennifer Givhan, Simone Muench, Christopher Theofanidis, and Chris Wise for taking time away from their own brilliant work to help shape this manuscript. *Dear Selection Committee* would not be what it is without you.

Many thanks to poet and artist extraordinaire, Karyna McGlynn, for the use of her collage, "It's Easy to Type," and for being a fantastic human in general.

Thanks, thanks, and more thanks to the strong, sassy, dazzling poets Dorothy Chan, Jennifer L. Knox, and Diane Seuss—your words mean so much to me.

Special thanks to Catherine Lu and Fran Sanders, who selflessly support Houston poets in countless ways.

Eternal gratitude to my family, for always being there for me— John Studdard, Lorrie Studdard, Kelly Studdard, Rosalind Williamson, Carolyn Carlson, and Peggy Ashkins.

And, finally, I'm so blessed to be walking the creative path with many kindred artist friends. There are far too many to name here, but I do want to say a special thanks to a few people whose support and encouragement meant a great deal to me during the

time I was writing the poems in this collection. Thank you
Ronda Piszk Broatch, Jeannine Hall Gailey, Patrick Harlin, Kelly
Iver, Lois P. Jones, R.J. Jeffreys, Paige Lewis, Anne Patterson,
Leslie Pietrzyk, Martha Silano, Pamela Uschuk, and the
Unnamed Collective (Ching-In Chen, Elena Gonzales Melinger,
Cassie Mira, Leslie Contreras Schwartz, Aliah Lavonne Tigh, and
Stalina Villarreal) for your art and inspiration and for being on
this journey with me.

JACKLEG PRESS

Brittney Corrigan
Jessica Cuello
Barbara Cully
Suzanne Frischkorn
Victoria Garza
Reginald Gibbons
D.C. Gonzales-Prieto
Neil de la Flor
Caroline Goodwin
Jennifer Harris
Meagan Lehr
Brigitte Lewis
D.K. McCutchen
Jean McGarry
Jenny Magnus
Rita Mookerjee
Mamie Morgan
cin salach
Maureen Seaton
Kristine Snodgrass
Cornelia Maude Spelman
Peter Stenson
Megan Weiler
David Wesley Williams

jacklegpress.org

CPSIA information can be obtained
at www.ICGtesting.com
Printed in the USA
LVHW050032250522
719627LV00008B/1570

9 781737 513414